A Transformative Bible Study
to Trash the Lies and Treasure the Truths

I0536263

Worthy

Know Your Worth and
Act Accordingly to Experience
Freedom, Enjoy Fulfillment,
and Live Fearlessly

The Worth Saving Series: Part 2

A Transformative Bible Study
to Trash the Lies and Treasure the Truths

Worthy

Know Your Worth and Act Accordingly to Experience Freedom, Enjoy Fulfillment, and Live Fearlessly

The Worth Saving Series: Part 2

Brenda A. Haire
and
Beth Madeline

Hardback ISBN: 978-1-956673-03-6
Paperback ISBN: 978-1-956673-02-9
Ebook ISBN: 978-1-956673-04-3
Library of Congress Control Number: 2022949074

Tips to Lead

Your First or Next
Bible Study

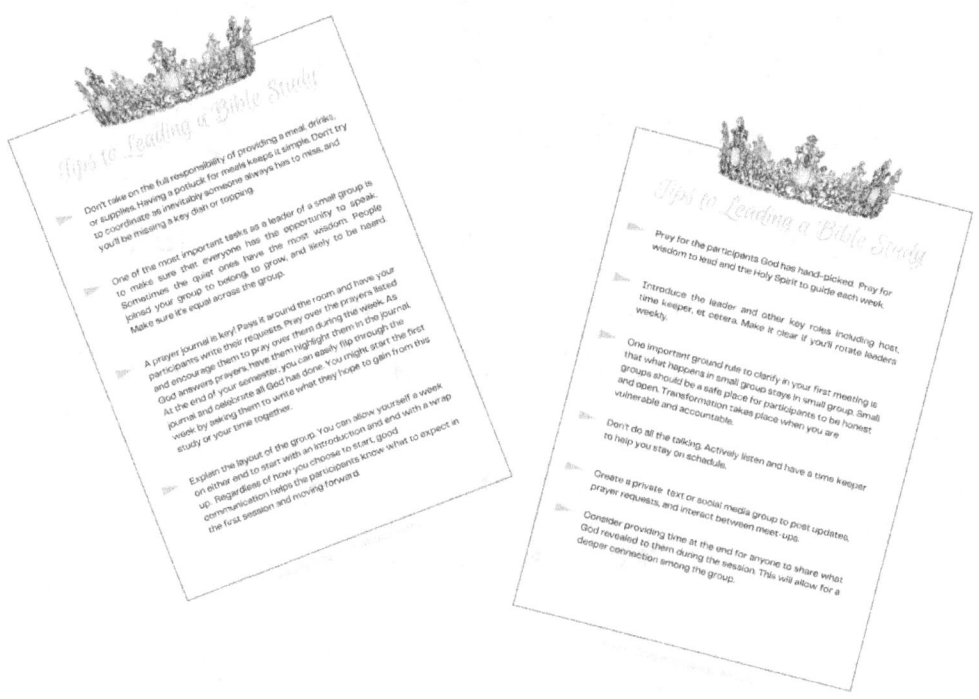

Download Yours Today

BrendaHaire.com/Bible-Study-Tips

Complete
The Worth Saving Series

Order copies for book clubs, small groups, and Bible classes at
BrendaHaire.com/Books

Other books by
Brenda A. Haire

Contents

Part 1: Trash the Lies

Part 2: Treasure the Truth

Part 3: Transform Your Life and Legacy

Draw Near

Welcome to a transformational Bible study based on the book *Save the Butter Tubs!: Discover Your Worth in a Disposable World* by me, Brenda A. Haire, the momma in this journey. I'm joined by my inspirational daughter, Beth Madeline. Our prayer is that through this study, you will see your true value. Whether you've read *Save the Butter Tubs!* before or not, we invite you to dive in to this study, get inspired, and let God's grace transform you.

You can make this an intimate fifteen-week study with just you, us, and the Lord. Alternatively, you can grab your girlfriends, sister, mother, Bible study group, et cetera, and make it a party. The accountability and discussions that come out of sharing this study with others are worth extending the invitation. If you choose to lead a group study, we've provided you with a guide in the back of this book.

During the next fifteen weeks, we will walk through the five lies we need to trash and the five truths we should treasure to transform our lives and legacy. Each week we will explore what God's Word says about these lies and discover how we can apply His Truth to our lives to experience a meaningful transformation that will impact generations.

You can work through each week's lesson in about thirty minutes. We reference most scriptures from the *New Living Translation* but invite you to use whichever translation is easiest for you to connect to God's heart. At the end of each lesson, you'll find a prayer prompt to start your conversation with God.

Grab your Bible and favorite pen, fill your cup of comfort—for Beth, iced coffee, and for Brenda, iced or hot tea depending on the time of year—and take a seat in the coziest spot you can find.

Ready, set, draw near.

Part 1

Trash the Lies

One

Lies We Eat: Creative Avoidance

Whatever you're called to do is more significant than any mess you've created to distract yourself from acting on it.
—from Chapter 1, *Save the Butter Tubs!*

~Brenda~

In 2003, I felt called to write. But instead of writing, I accepted several jobs, binge-watched television, ate too much, and thought about writing every day. In short, I became a master at creative avoidance.

Creative avoidance is a lot like procrastination—but with a twist that can be fatal to our dreams and legacies. *Procrastination* is the act of delaying or postponing work or action, knowing that we will *eventually* complete the task at hand. *Creative avoidance* is the act of delaying or postponing necessary action, knowing full well that, in doing so, we may *never* accomplish our goal. Creative avoidance takes effort and often includes erecting self-imposed obstacles that make moving forward all but impossible.

The biggest difference between procrastination and creative avoidance is commitment. When you commit to a project at work, you may procrastinate, but you will have to complete the task at some point. Without a deadline, you could creatively avoid the work forever. If there were no boundaries and you wouldn't get fired, you might never complete the project.

I didn't always avoid writing—just the scary parts. The parts that took faith. But I knew what God had called me to. I couldn't get away from the purpose He had placed on my heart and life. You can read more about my journey to finally becoming an author in *Save the Butter Tubs!*, the companion to this Bible study, but for now, know that overcoming creative avoidance has been one of the greatest challenges and blessings of my life.

I know I'm not alone. So many of us regularly and creatively avoid God's call on our lives—the very thing He has created and equipped us to do. Why? The answer is twofold. First, our God is a gracious God and doesn't give us the clear-cut deadlines our bosses do. God allows us to have free will. The second part of the answer is that we do this because we can't see the outcome, can't control it, and fear change and the unknown. Instead of using our free will to see His best for our lives, we use it to creatively avoid the unknown.

Which brings us to the *lies we eat*. Fear often manifests itself through overindulgence. If we eat this or buy that, we feel better. We find momentary satisfaction in the distraction from the fear we are feeling, the challenge of the unknown, or the discomfort of discipline necessary for obedience.

This week, we'll look at a couple whom God called to a unique purpose. I hope that after you complete the readings and reflections, you won't have room for creative avoidance, as your commitment to the calling on your life will be clearer, your faith stronger, and your hope renewed, truly transforming your life and legacy.

Read Genesis 15:1–21 (NLT).

In verse 4, what does God say Abram will have?

What is Abram asking for in verse 8?

Read Genesis 16:1–4 (NLT).

From Genesis 15:4 to 16:4, has God's plan for Abram changed?

How does Sarai take matters into her own hands?

Is the result favorable? Who does this affect? Explain.

Read Genesis 17:1–8 (NLT).

Has God's covenant with Abraham changed based on his actions with Hagar from Chapter 16? Why or why not?

How many times in verses 1–8 does God reaffirm His covenant with Abram with phrasing like, "I will," "I have," or "I may"?

Read Genesis 18:10–12 (NLT).

How did Sarah respond to God's call on her life?

In what ways have you responded in the past to God's call on your life?

Read Genesis 21:1–2 (NLT).

God's promises are real! He will follow through. He can make a way through our creative avoidance. What are you currently creatively avoiding?

Why are you avoiding it?

Consider this list of common creative avoidances and circle the ones you engage in most often.

Using drugs   Overeducating
Misusing alcohol   Using hobbies as an escape
Overeating   Socializing
Shopping   Napping
Engaging in unhealthy sexual activity   Reading
Watching television (or YouTube)   Changing jobs
Staying too busy   Other: _____

How do you feel God is responding to your creative avoidance?

Prayer

Father,

Forgive me for not acting on the call You've equipped me to fulfill. Help me see Your purpose for me clearly, have the faith to know You'll be with me, and the courage to take the first action in obedience.

I am worthy because...

Take a moment to write your prayer. Then use this space to reflect on this chapter. What has God's Word revealed to you?

Two

LIES WE BELIEVE: CONTROL

You need to decide—either you're god, or He is.
—from Chapter 2, *Save the Butter Tubs!*

~Beth~

In 2019, I worked on staff with an organization called Youth With A Mission (YWAM). One night after speaking on the phone about a worship school YWAM would host, I felt God next to me. "You're going to attend it," He said.

My immediate response was *no*. The school was for people who wanted to lead worship. Not only was this not my goal, but in my mind, I wasn't qualified. I didn't play any instruments, and the only time I sang was in the car or shower.

Even with all my reasons, saying no to God didn't sit well with me. I must have looked sad or discouraged sitting there thinking things over because a friend stopped and asked if I was okay. When I shared with her what I felt God told me, I said He would have to make it *very* clear if He wanted me to attend this school. I would need Him to confirm multiple ways. She asked, "How many times would God have to confirm?"

"Ten!" I responded.

Now I know what you might think: *Did she really challenge God?*

Yes, I did. I thought (hoped) that if I said a big enough number, He wouldn't provide, and I wouldn't have to go. I wanted to control the situation and didn't trust what God had planned for me.

I had underestimated God's persistence.

Minutes after I blurted out my challenge, another friend walked in the room—without knowing the situation—and spontaneously asked, "Beth, if you never step out of your comfort zone, how will you grow?" My heart sank. I knew God was speaking through her. In less than twenty-four hours, I had the additional nine confirmations from God.

The truth is, I was afraid. I was afraid I wouldn't be good enough, that people would judge me, or that somehow I would even disappoint God. None of that was true. YWAM's School of Worship challenged and stretched me in new ways. It was the best investment of my time because it brought me closer to who He wanted me to be. God knew it would be good for me, and it was. (You can read more about my YWAM experience in Chapter 7 of *Save the Butter Tubs!*)

Maybe you've felt God nudging you in a new direction, and, like me, you aren't convinced you want to say yes to His prompting. This week, we'll read a familiar story about someone else who tried to hide from God's call on his life.

Read Jonah 1:1–3 (ESV).

What is God asking Jonah to do?

How did Jonah respond to God?

Has God ever asked you to do something you didn't want to do? How did you respond?

Why don't you want to do what He's asking of you?

Read Jonah 2:9–3:10 (ESV).

What happened when Jonah let go of control?

What area of your life do you try to control the most?

What is holding you back from trusting God with that area of your life?

Prayer

Father,

Show me the areas of my life where I don't trust You or avoid what You are asking me to do. Help me trust You and Your Word in all areas of my life! I surrender control.

I am worthy because...

Take a moment to write your prayer. Then use this space to reflect on this chapter. What has God's Word revealed to you?

Three

Lies We Buy: Excess

The solution to this epidemic is simple, yet profound: understand your purpose, and you'll understand your needs.
—from Chapter 3, *Save the Butter Tubs!*

~Brenda~

C lothes, shoes, cars, gadgets, phones, apps, furniture,
houses . . . When is enough, *enough*? How much stuff
can we fill our homes with before we realize those things are
not filling us?

There's a reason the New Testament mentions money more
often than any subject other than the Kingdom of God. Our
relationship to money and the things we buy will affect our
daily lives. When we look at what Jesus has to say about
money, we see that living with excess is not our calling. And
no matter what or how much we buy, those *things* will never
make us the people God calls us to be. For that, we need
character.

In *Save the Butter Tubs!*, we look at how both character and
culture develop.

$$\text{Values} + \text{Action} = \text{Character}$$
$$\text{and}$$
$$\text{Values} + \text{Action} = \text{Culture}$$

Character develops in individuals. Culture develops in communities. And both character and the culture around us depend on *us*—what we value and how we behave. When we understand what we truly value, and our values align with our actions and beliefs, our character is authentic.

Let's pause here and look at the word *authentic*. When most people talk about being authentic, they mean that they strive to be the same on the inside as they are on the outside. This means if you're a mess on the inside and your house is a mess, you're authentic. That is *not* what we're talking about here.

According to the Google Dictionary, the true meaning of the word *authentic* is "of undisputed origin; genuine."

When your values and actions are in alignment, your character declares your origin. So let me ask you: Are you authentically the masterpiece God created you to be?

It's not enough to say we believe in Christ; we need to act on that belief. When we bury ourselves in excess, we are basically telling God that what He made isn't good enough and that we need all of this stuff around us to feel whole, valued, or important. *Ouch!* The next time you are on the verge of a binge or shopping spree, ask yourself what you truly value and what action would best represent your values.

If we focus more on what really matters—our relationship with our Savior, our family, the lost—our actions would be purposeful, and the need to fill the void with unnecessary stuff would dissipate. When the mission is clear, we can align everything in our lives to support it. Family, friends, and coworkers will take notice. That's how our character contributes to a culture in alignment with God's will.

Wouldn't you like to live in a culture where everyone is living out the values that they claim to hold dear? It starts with us.

Read 2 Chronicles 9:13–28 (NLT).

Don't skip verse 22. What are two things we know about Solomon?

What do you want to be known for? What do you want that dash on your headstone between your birth date and the day you return to Christ to represent?

Solomon's riches would be worth billions in today's market, but let's keep reading to see what he has to say about it.

Read Ecclesiastes 5:10–20 (NLT).

What does Solomon say about how we will arrive at the end of our life?

I don't know about you, but I want to die with an empty bank account. Not because I'm broke, but because I'm obedient.

Read 1 John 2:3–5 (NLT).

What does "knowing God" look like?

Read Matthew 6:19–21 (NLT).

What does Jesus say about our hearts?

Read Matthew 14:13–21 (NLT).

What did Jesus do with the little available?

Read John 10:10 (NLT).

What did Jesus say about His purpose?

In what ways is the thief robbing you of what Jesus wants for you?

Circle the things that Jesus provides you with an abundance of from the list below. Write in any others in the space provided.

Grace	Guidance	Self-control
Peace	Kindness	Faithfulness
Hope	Joy	Gentleness
Forgiveness	Patience	Himself
Love	Goodness	Provision

How can you multiply what God gave you for the Kingdom?

Prayer

Holy Spirit,

Show me the areas of my life that I'm filling with excess. Convict me with Your gentle ways so that I can break this fear-filled behavior and fill me with You instead.

I *am worthy because...*

Take a moment to write your prayer. Then use this space to reflect on this chapter. What has God's Word revealed to you?

Four

LIES WE TELL: EXCUSES

God sees the shadows in our lives, but He can also see what is hiding in them.

—from Chapter 4, *Save the Butter Tubs!*

~Beth~

When my momma asked me to pray about writing this Bible study with her, I thought, *I can't write a book. I've never even written more than a few pages for an English class. What would I write? I'm not qualified for this.*

Later, a childhood memory came to mind. When I was seven years old, I used printer paper from Momma's office, a pencil, some colors, and staples to craft a small princess book, which I then sold to a family friend for a dollar. I don't recall the contents of the book, but I remember being proud of my accomplishment.

With that memory, God reminded me that He made me in His image. I am creative because He is creative. That realization affirmed that if I coauthored a Bible study with Momma, it would also be a project that I do with Him. He would give me the words I needed to write.

I knew then that I could use the excuse, "I've never written a book; therefore, I am not qualified," or I could allow God to use me like I know He has used others throughout Scripture who would have considered themselves *unqualified*.

Read Exodus 4:1–12 (NIV).

What are your go-to excuses? Busy? Tired? Not educated enough? Unqualified?

Do you believe excuses are lies we tell ourselves and others? Explain your answer by defining excuses in your own words.

What lies are you telling yourself today?

God doesn't call the qualified but qualifies the called. In what ways do you feel disqualified to do what God is asking of you?

Read John 4:29 (NIV).

The woman at the well had excuses. How did she focus on God instead?

What truths will you focus on this week?

Prayer

Father,

Thank You that Your Word is true! Thank You for the examples throughout Your Word of equipping the unqualified. Help me see where I am making excuses and replace those excuses with Your Truth.

I am worthy because...

Take a moment to write your prayer. Then use this space to reflect on this chapter. What has God's Word revealed to you?

Five

LIES WE AVOID: FEAR

When you're fearful about your future, you are not including
God in your future.
—from Chapter 5, *Save the Butter Tubs!*

~Brenda~

All the lies we've discussed up to this point come down
to fear:

- We creatively avoid because we are afraid of the unknown, the outcome, or the work involved.

- Deceived by fear of change or the unknown, we attempt to control, believing that things will turn out
the way we planned if we are in control.

- We buy way too much based on either FOMO (fear
of missing out) or fear that we don't measure up. We
don't feel like we are enough the way God created us.

- We make excuses because we are afraid of the truth
and the unknown.

Fear contributes to a vicious cycle of creative avoidance, which causes us to feel bad about ourselves, and that causes us to binge on the creative avoidances listed in Week One. Then we make excuses for why we binge. (I'm sure you've heard the excuses from others. It's always easier to identify them when they come from someone else's mouth.)

The good news is that we can use fear in a healthy way—a way that causes us to pause and take steps in faith toward God rather than away from His purpose for our lives. The Bible tells us 365 times not to fear. Almost every one of those admonitions is accompanied by an encouragement (or command) to trust God.

God wants us to understand that He didn't call us to be fearful; God called us to be faithful.

Read Matthew 26:36–39 (NLT).

How did Jesus respond in the face of fear?

Why do you believe Jesus repeatedly told the disciples to keep watch and not give in to temptation?

Do you think fear is a sin? Why or why not?

When God tells us multiple times in Scripture not to fear, do you think He's giving a command or a suggestion?

Read James 4:17 (NLT).

What fears are keeping you from doing what you know you should be doing?

Why is it important that we not give in to fear?

More than thirty-two verses in the Bible mention fearing the Lord. What does it mean to fear God?

Read Psalm 112:1–10 (NLT).

These verses are full of promises. What is the key to receiving these promises?

Read Proverbs 2:1–11 (NLT).

What do these verses tell us to seek?

What will we receive in the process?

Read Proverbs 3:5–12 (NLT).

What do these verses tell us to seek?

What will we receive in the process?

Be sure to read Chapter 5 (pages 68–69) of *Save the Butter Tubs!* if you haven't.

Prayer

Father,

Thank You that You do not give us a spirit of fear and timidity, but of power, love, and self-discipline. Remind me of this when I reach for something other than the truth to confront my fears.

I am worthy because...

Take a moment to write your prayer. Then use this space to reflect on this chapter. What has God's Word revealed to you?

Before we move to the next part of this study, ask God what other lies you need to trash before you're able to treasure the truth. What is keeping you from the freedom He promises?

Part 2

Treasure the Truth

Six

BEGIN WITH INSPIRATION

Seeing a successful person, but not learning how they made it, is like seeing an oak tree and forgetting it was once an acorn.
—from Chapter 6, *Save the Butter Tubs!*

~Beth~

I graduated high school at sixteen years old with a semester of college under my belt. I continued my studies for another semester at a local junior college. During that time, I felt the Lord call me into full-time mission work. Following that calling would mean leaving college without a degree, letting go of everyone's expectations of me, and letting go of what I thought my life was going to look like.

Inspired by God's invitation, I transitioned to mission work with YWAM, but it wasn't easy. I felt the opposition of so many people who told me I should finish my college degree first. They said I wasn't qualified for missions—that I was too young.

Hearing those words over and over in my mind took a toll on my belief that I had the ability to do what I felt God had called me to do. I also felt like those people and their opinions put me in a box that felt too small and, at the same time, impossible to escape. To this day, I battle the beliefs planted by the enemy through others' words. I fear that I'm too young, that my story isn't powerful enough, and that my knowledge isn't as effective as others.

When I listen to what God tells me, however, I know those are all lies that the enemy wants me to believe, so I will stop talking about God and sharing my story. God has revealed to me again and again that He doesn't call the qualified, but He qualifies the called.

Read Matthew 9:9–13 (ESV).

What is one thing from your life that would surprise those around you?

In the past, what would you consider your disadvantages in life?

How could God be using those in your current situation? Are you allowing Him to?

Read Matthew 1:18–23 (ESV).

How was God in the story from the beginning?

Read Psalm 139:1–5, 13 (ESV).

How has God been in *your* story from the beginning?

Read Matthew 13:55, Mark 6:3, and Luke 3:23 (ESV).

Jesus was the son of a carpenter and a carpenter Himself until about thirty years old when He began His ministry.

What are some truths about Jesus' past that might surprise people?

Some truths to consider about Jesus:

- Born out of traditional wedlock

- Family tree had a few nuts

- Born among the barn animals

- Brother doubted His power

How do you think Jesus used His past for His ministry?

Prayer

Father,

Thank You that we don't have to have it all together to know You or to make You known. Thank You that Your plans for me are greater than the plans the world has in store.

I am worthy because...

Take a moment to write your prayer. Then use this space to reflect on this chapter. What has God's Word revealed to you?

Seven

BELONG IN YOUR WORLD

The gifts we have are an expression of love. They were given
in love, and we should give them away in love.
—from Chapter 7, *Save the Butter Tubs!*

~Brenda~

"Enjoy what you have rather than desiring what you don't have. Just dreaming about nice things is meaningless—like chasing the wind." Those words from Solomon in Ecclesiastes 6:9 (NLT) put life into proper perspective. It's easy to get so focused on the life we wish we had that we miss the blessings right in front of us.

Those blessings include our relationship with God and the way we see ourselves because of Him. When we shift our focus to enjoying our relationship with God and who He made us to be, we begin to care *less* about the minor worries of day-to-day life and *more* about the condition of our souls and the souls around us.

That shift starts with us and how we see our little world and ourselves. In Matthew 22 (NLT), Jesus commands, "Love your neighbor as yourself." But how do you love your neighbor while dissatisfied with yourself, your present situation, or the current condition of *your* soul?

A few years ago, I received an Instant Pot for my birthday. As someone who doesn't like to cook, I had big dreams for that small appliance. The problem was, no matter how many times I read the manual or pushed the buttons, I couldn't figure out how to use it. Eventually, I took it back to the store, but the sales clerk didn't want to take it back. I finally got store credit for an exchange, but the hassle almost wasn't worth it.

The experience reminded me of Jesus' exchange policy. He takes us back without question. It doesn't matter how damaged or used we are—He gladly accepts us. He made a full exchange for our souls before *we* realized we needed it.

The first step we can take toward loving ourselves is to surrender our lives to Jesus. Then we must forgive *ourselves* as He forgives us. He doesn't want us full of resentment, bitterness, self-doubt, and discontentment. He wants us to love ourselves *and* our neighbors.

Jesus is preparing a place for us that is unlike any place we can dream or imagine. Our time here is temporary. Let's not waste it wishing our world away. Belong. He is allowing you to be right where you are. Draw near to Him and walk with Him in the world's beauty He created.

If you haven't already taken a moment to surrender your life to Jesus, do so now. Pray (confess), thanking Jesus for forgiving you of your sins, and believe in your heart that He will, and He will save you. The exchange is that simple—our sin for His grace. No receipt required!

Read Luke 4:23–24 (NLT).

Describe a time you've felt out of place.

Describe your feelings when someone close to you has mocked or rejected you.

Read Luke 17:2–21 (NLT).

What do you think Jesus means in verse 21?

In what way is the Kingdom of God among us?

Read John 17:1–19 (NLT).

In verse 6, who does Jesus say the people belong to?

Now in verse 9, who is Jesus praying for and why?

What did He ask the Father for in verse 11?

In verse 13, what does Jesus want us to be filled with?

What did Jesus give them/us in verse 14?

Describe in your own words Jesus' prayer in verse 15.

What is Jesus acknowledging in verse 16?

What makes us holy, according to verse 17?

Verse 19 makes me weep. What emotions does it draw out of you and why?

Jesus gave Himself as a holy sacrifice for us so that God's Truth can make us holy. His physical earthly body may have left, but He equips us with God's Word, and we have the Holy Spirit living within us. The Kingdom is here! Until He decides, this is right where we belong.

Prayer

Jesus,

Thank You that You have not forsaken us. I pray the will of the Father to be done in and through me as I walk with You right where You've allowed me to be.

I *am worthy because...*

Take a moment to write your prayer. Then use this space to reflect on this chapter. What has God's Word revealed to you?

Eight

Believe in Your Dreams

Don't be afraid to readjust. As you grow, so will your dreams.
—from Chapter 8, *Save the Butter Tubs!*

~Brenda~

What dreams do you have (or have you had) for your life? What obstacles have crept in and prevented those dreams from becoming a reality? Jot down the obstacles that have either crept in the way of your dreams or are blocking you from remembering them at all.

When I sought my purpose, I recalled the advice of many well-meaning gurus to remember what you liked to do as a child. This recommendation would stop me in my tracks every time. I recall little of my childhood. I have a pretty spotty memory, period. As a published author and publishing consultant, I shake my head at this advice even more. As a child, I didn't like books. I failed reading in the third grade. I also failed typing in high school. I *did* enjoy my high school English classes and loved to write essays but would have never linked that to a future career opportunity.

I recall many, many trips to bookstores as a tween with my mom. I hated those trips, and I couldn't understand her love of books. I'd hang out in the magazine section until she did her shopping. At age nineteen, I read a book by choice for the first time. Then, I began discovering genres I enjoyed and how books can open the mind and heart.

My dream of writing developed out of obedience to what God called me to do. It wasn't a desire I had early on. Before the age of thirty, when I first felt called to write, I would have laughed at the thought of being a published author and a publishing consultant.

We can't always see what God has planned for us. I struggled in obedience to write that first book. Never in my wildest dreams would I have seen this one coming. But God!

Our dreams are from God. He created you, and He hasn't forgotten the plans He has for you. He knows how to weave together all the things you've discounted in your life and work them for your good. To use your gifts well, you need to align yourself with God. Don't doubt the Designer. Don't get ahead of Him either. Draw close and allow Him to reveal the actions. Take them. Even the small ones. He won't lead you astray.

Read Genesis 37:5–11 (NLT).

What were Joseph's brothers' responses to his dreams?

Why do you think they responded this way?

Why do you believe Joseph shared his dream with his family?

Do you think he should have kept his dream to himself? Why or why not?

Our dreams are personal. Whom can you trust with your dreams?

Read Genesis 22:1–18 (NLT).

To say this command was huge would be an understatement. Has God ever asked you to do something that felt bigger than you? What did He ask, and how did you respond?

What do you think God was testing in Abraham?

Share about a time you feel you failed one of God's tests.

How do you think He can still use your failure to accomplish His plan?

How can your past failure shape your story or testimony?

Prayer

Father God,

Thank You for believing in me and providing a dream in my heart. Please provide clarity as I take action, wisdom while I walk with You, and provision to reach the people You'd have me reach.

I am worthy because...

Take a moment to write your prayer. Then use this space to reflect on this chapter. What has God's Word revealed to you?

Nine

BLOOM IN RELATIONSHIPS

Don't make it so hard for God to use you."
—from Chapter 9, *Save the Butter Tubs!*

~Brenda~

Let's be real: Relationships take effort because people are messy. Relationships also require intentionality. Just as our Creator Himself intentionally created Adam and Eve for the first relationship, we need to be intentional about our relationships—first with Him, second with those He has entrusted to us. God made us for connection with Him and with one another.

Imagine walking and talking to God in the garden. No shame, just exploring creation with the Creator. Now your mind may have jumped to the Garden of Eden, but there is no reason we can't have this same walk and talk with God today. He is with you. He wants to be in a relationship with you.

As we grow in our relationship with God, our earthly relationships will deepen. We will begin to see others the way God sees them and to see ourselves the way He sees us.

As Jesus suffered, nailed to the cross, the prayers He offered provide us three keys to relationships:

    1. Communication

    2. Forgiveness

    3. Sacrifice

Communication

"My God, My God, why hast thou forsaken me?"
—Matthew 27:46 (KJV), Mark 15:34 (KJV)

In this raw cry, we learn that communication should be honest. It's best to be open about our needs, sharing from the depth of our hearts and not just surface chatter.

Our communication should also acknowledge who the other person is to us, honoring their position in our life.

Our communication with God happens through prayer and actions. Someone once asked me, "Why do we pray if God knows everything?" He already knows the condition of our hearts. Praying acknowledges our relationship with Him and honors who He is in our lives.

Unlike God, the people in our lives don't know what we are thinking or how we are feeling. We have to risk being open if we are going to deepen our relationships with them. As we share our thoughts and feelings with our friends or spouse, that communication acknowledges who they are and honors the role they play in our lives.

Read Matthew 6:9–13 (ESV).

Fill in the blanks verse by verse.

Verse 9

When we follow this example, we are acknowledging _____ and He is in _____. His name is _____.

Verse 10

We are asking for His _____ to come and His _____ to be done. How?

Verse 11

How often do we want provision?

Verse 12

He is acknowledging our _____ and the _____ of others against us. What are we to do?

Verse 13

What are we asking for protection from?
Some translations finish verse 13 by honoring God in what way?

Forgiveness

> From His humble position on the cross, Jesus prays, "Father, forgive them; for they know not what they do." —Luke 23:34 (KJV)

Unforgiveness hurts us and those around us, and rarely does the person we are holding in contempt even realize how we feel. Do you think the people crucifying Jesus realized what they were doing? Explain.

Read Matthew 6:14–15 (ESV).

You were probably familiar with verses 6–13, but we usually stop short of 14–15 in most corporate worship services.
  What's the big "if?"

Read Matthew 18:31–35 (ESV).

What are the consequences of unforgiveness from our Heavenly Father?

Sacrifice

> And with these words, Jesus breathed His last breath: "Father, into thy hands I commend my spirit." —Luke 23:46 (KJV)

The most important relationship in our lives should be with our Savior. Most people would probably sacrifice for their children, close family members, or friends—simple sacrifices like giving up your favorite spot on the couch or eating dinner at their favorite spot instead of yours. But Jesus is asking us to take up our cross.

Read Luke 9:23–27 (ESV).

What does it mean to take up our cross?

How often does Jesus tell us we must take up our cross?

What happens if we try to hang on to our lives?

How do we save our lives?

Rate yourself on a scale from one to ten on how you are doing in these three areas with Jesus.

Communication

1 2 3 4 5 6 7 8 9 10

Forgiveness

1 2 3 4 5 6 7 8 9 10

Sacrifice

1 2 3 4 5 6 7 8 9 10

Now, rate yourself on a scale from one to ten on how you are doing with your closest friends and family in these three areas.

Communication

1 2 3 4 5 6 7 8 9 10

Forgiveness

1 2 3 4 5 6 7 8 9 10

Sacrifice

1 2 3 4 5 6 7 8 9 10

Write your best next steps to improve in any areas that need your attention.

Prayer

Heavenly Father,

Thank You for creating me to be in a relationship with You. Help me believe who You say I am. Help me show up in the lives of others with open communication, forgiveness, and sacrifice.

I am worthy because...

Take a moment to write your prayer. Then use this space to reflect on this chapter. What has God's Word revealed to you?

Ten

BREATHE IN EXPERIENCES

Focusing on the trial would be like focusing on the caterpillar's experience of living in the dark cocoon or the trouble he has breaking out of it instead of focusing on the beautiful wings and strength he has gained.
—from Chapter 10, *Save the Butter Tubs!*

~Beth~

When preparing for School of Worship, I felt like God wanted me to raise support so I could focus on the mission work He had asked me to do rather than focus on earning a paycheck. This was a hard concept for me to accept, as I came from a hardworking family, and the idea of asking for money rather than earning it felt strange. It was a busy season. I was working at YWAM and preparing to start the worship school—all while fundraising—leaving little time to develop deep friendships.

One day, I was working in the dorm at YWAM, and I had a huge craving for a specialty coffee from our local shop. I was tight on money, though, so I knew dropping five dollars on a coffee wasn't practical. A few minutes after thinking about my craving, my friend Hope walked into the dorm and said, "Hey, Beth, I want to buy you a coffee." Her offer brought me to tears. Later she told me she wasn't aware of my craving or my financial situation. She simply wanted to do something kind for me—and she knew coffee was my love language!

I knew that coffee craving was silly, but God used a sweet friend to provide for my desire as a gentle reminder that He specializes in the details and cares about relationships. The time I got to spend with Hope as we enjoyed our drinks was sweeter than the coffee. More than that, the memory I have of how God used her to bless me in a simple way is something I won't forget.

Read John 10:10 (ESV).

What abundance is Jesus talking about?

What is the truth about the enemy Jesus speaks of?

What does God give us an abundance of?

Read Matthew 5:14–16 (ESV).

In *Save the Butter Tubs!*, Momma reminds us, "You are a light on the hill. Don't let your previous experiences or current circumstances be the lampshade that hides your light."

What current circumstances are hindering your light from shining for all to see?

How do you see God shining in the small details of your life?

Prayer

Thank You, Lord, that You know the desires of our hearts, no matter how big or small. Thank You that You provide for every need. Help me to be intentional with my time and my relationships.

I am worthy because...

Take a moment to write your prayer. Then use this space to reflect on this chapter. What has God's Word revealed to you?

Before we move to the next part of this study, ask God what if there are specific truths He wants you to focus on as you intentionally leave your legacy.

Part 3

Transform Your Life and Legacy

Eleven

Expand Your Faith

"If you don't believe in your dreams, you begin to tear your-self down. You find ways to avoid what your heart is calling you to do."
—from Chapter 11, *Save the Butter Tubs!*

~Beth~

If you've read Chapter 11 in *Save the Butter Tubs!*, you've read about God calling me into full-time missions with YWAM. My first step was to attend Discipleship Training School (DTS).

The week before the DTS started, I wondered whether I should wait and attend the next school scheduled to start two months later. God knew what He was doing when He prompted my pastor to call and encourage me with the affirmation that God was going to provide for my school. I decided not to wait and had faith that God would provide everything I needed for the DTS. Three days before the school started, the Lord provided all of the money needed to attend. Later, I learned that they canceled the next session, and I would not have been able to attend.

Again, when it was time for the mission outreach portion of DTS, when we were to travel to Colombia, I was short on funds. I thought, *If I don't go now, maybe I can get the money together and go later*. Once again, the Lord provided all that I needed for the outreach in just three days. This was when I concluded that if God can raise Jesus from the dead in three days, He can provide for me in three days.

Later, when working as a staff member with YWAM, a friend asked me during a worship night, "What are three things I could pray for that would push you further in what you feel God is calling you to do? These things could be hindrances, fears, resources, et cetera." The question challenged me to think about what was holding me back, what I had been fixing my mind on, and what I needed to pray and trust for more.

> "For we walk by faith, not by sight." —2 Corinthians
> 5:7 (ESV)

I asked my colleague to pray that God would expand my faith. Looking back, I can see how the Lord has provided, and yet, like many others, I still have my doubts from time to time. He made the impossible possible. My prayer then—and now—is that God will help me trust Him first and always.

Read Philippians 4:6–8 (ESV).

What are you worrying about?

What does Paul tell us to fix our thoughts on?

List three things you could pray for that would push you further in what you feel God is calling you to do.

List three things you are thankful God has done for you. Tell Him.

Prayer

Father God,

I'm thankful You continue to expand my faith. Thank You that You have placed people in my life to pull me from my racing mind and to challenge my daily thoughts. Help me continue to trust You and fix my eyes on You.

I am worthy because...

Take a moment to write your prayer. Then use this space to reflect on this chapter. What has God's Word revealed to you?

Twelve

ENGAGE NEW STORIES

You have the freedom to control the narrative that plays in your head. If you don't like the story you are telling yourself, be brave and change the ending. Remember, some chapters of your life are worth rereading, and others need to be edited. We know you can't change the past, but you can change the story you tell yourself about the past.
—from Chapter 12, *Save the Butter Tubs!*

~Beth~

In high school, students bullied and even assaulted me. We were new to a small town, and I didn't fit in with their cliques. Those factors combined with how some students treated me made me feel less than those around me—unworthy, isolated, and powerless.

I could choose to live with that story and blame myself or my circumstances for what happened to me. Or I can choose to write a new story based on the truth and freedom found in my Savior. You can probably guess that I chose to do the latter.

Now, when I tell myself the story of my high school years, I truly feel sorry for the people who caused me pain. My heart breaks for them because I know that hurt people, hurt people. Hurt, jealous, insecure, and trying to prove their worth, they treated me awfully. It's sad that they felt powerful in the moments when they were hurting me—sad that the times they felt powerful were when others felt powerless. That's not power at all. That's abuse.

We find true power in meekness, self-control, and kindness. True power comes from the Holy Spirit.

Write the last thoughts you had about yourself.

How would you feel if your friends spoke to you like that?

Take a moment to think about how God sees you. What do you think He sees?

Read Psalm 139:14, 17–18 (ESV).

He sees you as fearfully and wonderfully made. He made you in *His* image. What does that look like to you?

Today, because I know how God sees me, I can walk forward and change what I speak over myself. This isn't a one-time fix. There are days when I have to choose to remind myself what God says about me. Therefore, I keep what Momma refers to as a Victory Channel©.

A Victory Channel is a list you write of the experiences where God has shown Himself mightily. These are things I feel God has done for me, ways He has protected me, encouragement He has spoken to me, or instances in which I can't explain the miracle that has occurred. God brings me renewed courage and power when I remember and reflect on what He has done.

Read Joshua 4:4–7 (ESV).

What were these stones chosen to do?

Read Isaiah 30:8 (ESV).

What is the point of writing these things down?

What is a story in your life that could use some rewriting?

What truth will you now tell yourself about that story?

In *Save the Butter Tubs!*, Momma describes what she calls your Victory Channel. You need to change the channel in your mind to play the victories God has already provided in your life instead of staying on the channel playing the story that is not serving you well.

Start your Victory Channel here by writing three to five moments that you know God had His hand in events, circumstances, or provision in your life. It doesn't have to be something huge; God is in even the smallest of details. Refer to this list often and add to it every chance you get. When you feel fear or doubt creeping in, when your faith wavers, remember what God has already done in your life. As the third part in this *Worth Saving Series*, Momma has written a guided journal with 365 prompts to help you capture the goodness of God and focus on what He has done in your life. I highly encourage you to get a copy, if not now, when you are finished with this study, to continue to focus on the power of God in your life.

Write three to five victories.

Prayer

Lord,

I thank You now for the story You have for my life. Help me when I forget who I am in You. Thank You for Your forgiveness. I forgive those who have hurt me. I trust You and the plans You have for me, even when I can't see the next step.

I *am worthy because...*

Take a moment to write your prayer. Then use this space to reflect on this chapter. What has God's Word revealed to you?

Thirteen

Embrace a Routine

Transformation happens when you're the most frag-
ile—you're trusting in faith and can't control what's about to
take place.
—from Chapter 13, *Save the Butter Tubs!*

~Brenda~

I'm an adventurous person—quick to try new things and
take risks. Having *routines* always sounded boring to me.
I thought they wouldn't allow for the freedom I wanted to
enjoy. *Discipline* is another word that always made me cringe.
I didn't have many rules growing up, so making rules for
myself didn't sound appealing.

For years, I struggled to create a schedule that fit my goals.
My mindset changed, however, when my goal finally aligned
with my purpose. Once purpose consumed me, routine became a necessity. Discipline also became a way of life when I
realized that my personal discipline affects my influence and
impact on those with whom God has entrusted me.

The root word of discipline is *disciple*. Let that sink in. Take
a moment to jot down how you see the correlation between
these two words.

Discipline

Disciple

To be a disciple means to be a follower. It's not wrong, it just depends who or what you're following. Not having a routine could mean we are following our own sinful nature. Or it could mean we are trying to control our circumstances or not let others control us.

If you are a disciple of Jesus—a follower of Christ—you are following the right person. And following Him isn't about being controlled; it's a choice.

Many people don't feel qualified to be a disciple of Jesus, but remember: He does the qualifying. He will equip you with provisions every step of your journey.

When Jesus gathered the first disciples, He chose very ordinary men. He required them to drop what they were doing and follow Him. That's it. No college degree required. No exam to pass or school to attend. The only test was willingness. Are you willing?

List what you need to drop to make room for Jesus in your life.

Maybe you're saying to yourself right now, *I have Jesus in my life, lady! I'm doing this Bible study.* I'd then ask you to make a list of what you need to drop to follow God's call on your life. First, identify the call. What is God calling you to do that you are allowing creative avoidance, fear, and other distractions to keep you from?

Now, list the obstacles in the way of obedience to your calling.

Hear my heart: Don't create a routine of going to church only to check the weekly box for following Jesus. We *should* go to church and gather with other believers (Hebrews 10:25). That absolutely should be part of our routine. Still, if that is the only time you're following Jesus, I'd ask if you're truly following Him. Because you're taking part in this Bible study and have made it to Week Thirteen, I'm pretty sure you're truly seeking Christ and all that He has for you. It won't always be easy, but it will always be worth it.

Read Mark 1:35–39 (ESV).

What did Jesus do first?

Where did He do this?

Why do you think Jesus started His day this way?

What does verse 38 say about Jesus' mission?

In what ways will having a clear mission help you establish a better routine?

Describe the outcome if Jesus hadn't stayed on mission (verse 39).

Prayer

Dear Jesus,

Thank You for showing me how important it is to stay focused on the mission set before me. Thank You for allowing me to come to You for clarity and rest, reflect on my true priorities, and make Your desires my own.

I am worthy because...

Take a moment to write your prayer. Then use this space to reflect on this chapter. What has God's Word revealed to you?

Fourteen

Elevate Your Influence

If we're focusing on what we think others should or shouldn't be doing, then we're not focused on what God wants us to do.

—from Chapter 14, *Save the Butter Tubs!*

~Beth~

When I was fifteen years old, I ran away from home. I was depressed and angry and certain no one would care if I left. So I got in a car with strangers and ended up on the other side of town. It wasn't long before a cop found me and brought me home.

I was terrified that once home, I'd get yelled at or severely punished for my actions. Not because of anything my parents did, but out of what I was telling myself I deserved. I remember that night sitting in Momma's lap like a kid as she held me and loved me.

Every action (positive or negative) has a consequence. My parents could have fired me up with punishment and let out their hurt and anger on me, but they didn't. Instead, they loved me harder, held me tighter, and listened with intentionality. Little did I know that night, their response would have so much influence, not only on how I moved forward, but on how I saw God. That memory of Momma holding me is how I see God holding us when we are hurting, angry, and in trouble.

It is easy for us to find fault or imperfection in one another; it's hard to embrace that God created every individual in His image. I once heard this quote, "The ability to perceive faults in another is a cheap and common gift." God calls us to be encouragers in and to the body of Christ. This means sharpening one another with the Word of God, holding each other accountable, and loving one another as Christ loves us.

Can you see God when you look at others? Are you looking for ways to encourage others—lifting them up and holding them close when they are hurting?

No matter how young or old you are, you have influence on someone in your life. You may know them or not; they could be a stranger in passing or your closest friend. To elevate your influence, you must be wise in how you lead, respond, and give advice. And like Momma was with me when I ran away, you have to be intentional with kindness and grace.

Your influence is powerful. Don't abuse it, and don't waste it.

Read Luke 15:11–32 (ESV).

How would you have responded to this situation?

Do you think the son embarrassed and angered his father? If so, in what ways?

How did the father react to his son's homecoming?

Jesus told this parable the way He did because this is how our Heavenly Father reacts to our homecoming, no matter what we've done. He rejoices when His kids turn to Him. Luke 15:7 (ESV) says, "Just so, I tell you, there will be more joy in heaven over one sinner who repents than over ninety-nine righteous persons who need no repentance".

Prayer

Father,

Help me use my influence to point people toward You. Help me to respond in love and patience rather than in anger and frustration.

I am worthy because...

Take a moment to write your prayer. Then use this space
to reflect on this chapter. What has God's Word revealed to
you?

Fifteen

ENHANCE YOUR LEGACY

Your story matters. The role you play in the
stories of others matters.
—from Chapter 15, *Save the Butter Tubs!*

~Brenda~

R ecently in church, I wept as a song I had never heard
filled the sanctuary. Tears streamed down my face as
I imagined how my friend Joe, one of my cheerleaders for
writing and teaching God's Word, would have loved this song.
The Blessing by Kari Jobe featuring Cody Carnes released in
2020. The lyrics are from Joe's favorite Bible verse, Numbers
6:24–26 (NIV):

> "The Lord bless you and keep you; the Lord make
> his face shine on you and be gracious to you; the
> Lord turn his face toward you and give you peace."

After many years of suffering with health issues, our Heavenly Father called Joe home in December 2020. Through the
tears, I thought of all the lives Joe touched. I'm blessed to
have called him a friend.

This is such a simple remembrance of a man that, through all of his suffering, still clung to our Lord, our church family, and the promises of God. His faith is what we will remember about him. That is his legacy.

What will your legacy be? If you feel uncomfortable thinking about your legacy, I understand. Caring about your legacy can seem self-serving, and it is if your motives aren't in the right place. But when you walk closely with God, as Joe did, His desires will become your desires—not just for the short term but for your entire life. Philippians 2:13 (NLT) tells us,

> "For God is working in you, giving you the desire
> and the power to do what pleases him."

If we are intentional about our relationship with God, we are intentional about our legacy. We will focus on eternal rewards and not the things that will rot and rust.

Legacies are about responses. Let me say that again: *Legacies are about responses.* I know Joe had unbearable days, but through it all, he still loved God, believed for good, and wanted the best for those around him.

How we respond to Jesus and how we respond to the call on our lives will absolutely leave a legacy. How we respond to those around us, the world tugging at our souls, our children when they misbehave, the rude clerk, the guy that cut us off in traffic while our children sit observing in the back seat will all be part of our legacy. It is our response to the life Jesus has given us that leaves legacies.

How will you respond?

Read Deuteronomy 30:15–20.

What options sit before us?

What are we commanded to do?

Write the blessings that come from obedience.

What types of gods or idols are you allowing to turn your heart away from this commandment?

What are the consequences of disobeying?

In verse 19, whom does your obedience affect?

How is your life described in verse 20?

Read 1 Corinthians 13:4–13 (NLT).

What three things will last forever?

Write tangible ways you can show these three things to others.

Prayer

Lord God,

Thank You that You are my life. Help me express my faith in ways that others can see my love for You. Forgive me where I have fallen short in loving You and those around me. Please guide me as I choose the abundant life You offer and help me leave a legacy that will have an eternal impact.

I am worthy because...

Take a moment to write your prayer. Then use this space to reflect on this chapter. What has God's Word revealed to you?

Group Leader Guide

Congratulations for taking the step of obedience in leading a Bible study! Whether this is your first time or your thousandth, we applaud you. Leading can be lonely and often unappreciated, but we want you to know you are not alone. The Holy Spirit will be with you each step of the way! We appreciate you, and your rewards will be great in Heaven.

Pray

Start praying the minute you decide to lead this study. Pray for the participants God has hand-picked. Pray for your own transformation and protection as you lead. Before each session, pray for wisdom to lead and the Holy Spirit to guide each week. Pray after your participants leave. This is when the enemy likes to come after leaders. Remember, God called you to lead. Don't let the enemy discourage you. God wastes nothing. Open each session in prayer and end each session with prayer.

Online, in Person, or Hybrid

In our rapidly changing world, many formerly in-person groups are now meeting online. You can do this study the same way. Make it work for your community. If you meet online, set ground rules for everyone to follow. Have them all turn their cameras on. If you're going to build an intimate group, you need to see one another's faces. Have them mute themselves until they are speaking so that any background noise will not be a distraction. Ask that they attempt to meet from a quiet, well-lit place.

If meeting over a meal would make people more comfortable, you can still do this in person or online. If online, everyone can come with their meal prepared, or you could do a potluck if meeting in person. Again, make it work for your community.

Set Up for Success

Explain the ground rules from the beginning. Don't spend too much time or harp on one rule in particular, but set up your group with expectations. Keep it in a friendly tone and be transparent in your desire to see true transformation.

One important ground rule to clarify from your first meeting is that what happens in small group stays in small group. Small groups should be a safe place for participants to be honest and open. Share this with your group and let them know that you truly want to see transformation take place, and that only happens when everyone feels comfortable being themselves. Remind participants not to talk about what they discuss with other groups, friend circles, or at church.

Prayer Journals

A prayer journal is a powerful tool when leading small groups, and it's a necessity in larger groups. If you were to take prayer requests in a group of twelve, you could be there all night—which wouldn't be a bad thing at all, just not the original purpose for your gathering.

A prayer journal can be a blank notebook or a small journal. Pass it around the room and have your participants write their requests. You can pray over the prayers listed and encourage them to pray over those prayers written in the journal during the week. Each week, as God answers prayers, have them highlight them in the journal. At the end of your semester together, you can easily flip through the journal and celebrate all God has done. You might start the first week by asking them specifically to write what they hope to gain from this study or your time together.

Everyone Participates

One of the most important tasks as a leader of a small group is to make sure that everyone has the opportunity to speak. Sometimes the quiet ones have the most wisdom. You want to hear from everyone, and it's your job to wrangle in the talkative participants, so the introverts have a chance to speak. It's also your job to stay on point and not let someone derail the conversation. If you have one overly talkative person monopolize the conversation every time you meet, your group will dwindle quickly. People joined your group to belong, to grow, and likely to be heard. Make sure it's equal across the group.

Dig In

Your group may wish to read *Save the Butter Tubs!: Discover Your Worth in a Disposable World* together while going through the study. To purchase bulk copies, email Speakto Me@BrendaHaire.com with the subject: Bulk Copy Order.

Regardless of whether participants have read *Save the Butter Tubs!*, this study can be transformative. The study is fifteen weeks. You can allow yourself a week on either end to start with an introduction or wrap-up. I prefer to dive right in, as that is why most people join a group. No matter which way you choose to start, notify the participants of what to expect in the first session. Let them know if they need to come prepared with the first session completed and the introduction and first chapter of *Save the Butter Tubs!* read, or if they should bring their study, and you'll dive in together. Communication will be the key to bring everyone together for a great first session.

Be sure to keep in mind why people joined the journey with you and value their time and purpose.

Options

1. Read *Save the Butter Tubs!* together and work through the study as a group. Have them read beforehand so the group can discuss both the reading and the study during your sessions. For additional discussion questions, you can grab the free Club Guide at Bren daHaire.com/bookclub.

1. Participants complete each session before meeting then discuss when together. As the leader, you'll walk them through the questions in each session and discuss them along the way.

2. Read aloud during the group session and allow time as each member completes the questions. Then discuss.

If you choose to lead a group discussion, we'd love to hear about it. Please join us in our Facebook community and let us know: Facebook.com/groups/aworthybookclub.

Acknowledgments

We thank God for giving us this opportunity to share about His goodness and grace. We are humbled and honored.

Brenda's

Beth, thank you for holding me accountable for writing this Bible study by taking the journey with me. Your faith and dreams inspire me to continue to live big! I love you and am blessed to be your momma.

I am forever thankful for my hubs, Darren, who never stands in the way of God's call on my life, reminds me to stay focused, and believes in my wildest dreams. I love you and am thankful for the way you love me and our beautifully blended family.

Shine Tyler for your support and use of your space. LifePoint Fellowship Church and Pastor Alex Velarde for your continued support.

Beth's

I'd like to thank Momma for including me on this journey. It has been a journey of emotions, healing, growth, and memories that I will forever cherish. I am blessed and honored to be your daughter. You inspire me daily, Momma. I love you.

About the Authors

After graduating high school at sixteen, Beth served as a missionary for two and a half years. During this time, she realized her passion for sharing truth with young people through writing, teaching, and speaking.

Beth enjoys being active in the gym, adventuring to new coffee shops, and spending time with her pup, Isa. Beth is also a spontaneous soul like her momma.

Brenda, who has been working since she was twelve years old, has held more than forty jobs. She's never been fired and is not ashamed of her diverse work history, having always worked her way up, out, and on to the next adventure. Many see this as risky, and some would call her fearless. She would tell you that fear was always a factor; she just chose faith instead.

After being told she was a nobody by a publisher, Brenda struggled with her identity as a writer. Not one to give up, she pursued her dream and released her first book, *Save the Butter Tubs!: Discover Your Worth in a Disposable World* in 2018.

Brenda was immediately hired by her publishing agency after her book was released, and she went on to become the president of the company. An entrepreneur at heart, once again she left on top and now uses her experience to serve individuals and small businesses around the world as the CEO and co-founder of Joy of Pursuit. Brenda created the Author Business Network with her business partner, Amanda Painter, and together they help authors build businesses around their books and business owners position themselves with a book and solid HR practices.

As a speaker, Brenda shares keynotes and workshops that transform audiences. Whether she is speaking about purpose, publishing, or human resources, her deepest desire is to help you shine your light by operating in your grace-given gifts. It's not enough that you see her light; you need to see your own. As Brenda says, "It's there. You're valuable. Your story matters." She considers herself a "moved soul"—so moved by her encounters with God that she can't help but move in response. She wants the same for you—to encounter God in a way that you can't help but live a life worthy of your calling.

Brenda and her "hubs" (as she lovingly refers to him on social media), Darren, are both military veterans. They enjoy hiking and chasing waterfalls across the United States and live in Texas with their beautifully blended family and loyal Jack Russell, Maggie.

Connect at BrendaHaire.com

What Keeps You from Living on Purpose with Freedom, Fulfillment, and Focus?

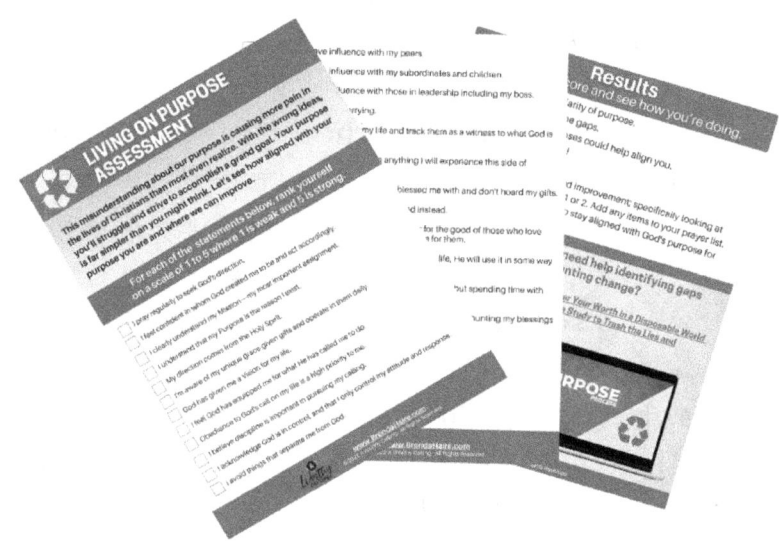

Take the
Living on Purpose
Assessment

BrendaHaire.com/Purpose-Assessment

Not sure how to walk in your purpose daily?

Let Brenda guide you to live and work on purpose through
The Purpose Process Course.
Start living the life you are called to.

BrendaHaire.com/Purpose-Process-Course

STAY CONNECTED

Brenda shares monthly resources and reminders to support you as you live and work on purpose. Get yours at BrendaHaire.com.

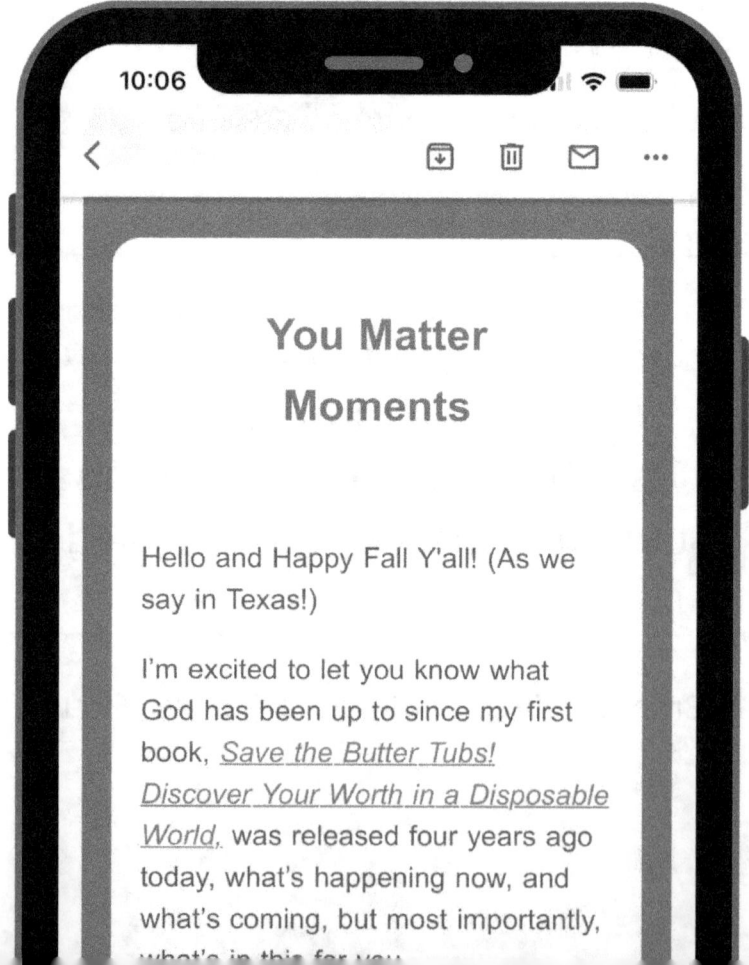

You Matter Moments

Hello and Happy Fall Y'all! (As we say in Texas!)

I'm excited to let you know what God has been up to since my first book, *Save the Butter Tubs! Discover Your Worth in a Disposable World,* was released four years ago today, what's happening now, and what's coming, but most importantly, what's in this for you.

Buy in Bulk or in Sets

For Your Small Groups, as Gifts,
or for Event Participants.

BrendaHaire.com/Shop

Thank you!

Help others trash the lies and treasure
the truths by leaving a review for this
Bible study on Amazon or your other
favorite online book retailer. Brenda
personally reads and appreciates each
review. Thank you for your support in her
effort to glorify God through her writing.

Looking for a Speaker?

Keynotes - Workshops - Retreats

Brenda is a sought-after speaker. Her passion to guide individuals to operate in their grace-given gifts will inspire and empower your audience.

Start the conversation at
BrendaHaire.com/Speaker

www.ingramcontent.com/pod-product-compliance
Lightning Source LLC
Chambersburg PA
CBHW071205120626
46546CB00006B/2425